# Read A Rhyme, Write A Rhyme

Poems selected by
## Jack Prelutsky

Illustrated by **Meilo So**

if were a bu
not

a giat be

no

Alfred A. Knopf
New York

# A Letter from Jack

Hi, kids.

For almost forty years, I've been writing dozens of books of poems for you, something that I've always had lots of fun doing. I've also compiled anthologies, which are collections of other people's poems (along with a few of my own) for you to enjoy. The book you are reading now is also an anthology, but it's a bit different from any I've done before. In this collection, I'm inviting you to take part in the writing process, and I'm giving you a head start to help you create your own poems.

A few years ago, several Web sites invited me to come up with some poetry activities that children and teachers all over the country could take part in. I came up with "poemstarts," in which I would begin poems with two to six lines, then invite everyone to continue and even finish them. This turned out to be such a popular idea that I couldn't keep up with the responses. I expected that maybe fifty or a hundred kids would post their poems on the Web site, but I ended up getting thousands and thousands of poems from students and their teachers.

I remember that one of the poemstarts went like this:

**Every day when I go out,**
**I stuff my shoes with sauerkraut.**

I was astonished by how many people enjoyed continuing this poemstart, and was delighted and impressed by the creativity they demonstrated. In some cases, I thought the continuations were better and funnier than my own ideas. It was then that I thought that doing a whole collection of poemstarts might be a fine idea for a book.

I've taken the idea a bit further here. I've selected poems that I like on ten different topics, three poems apiece. Then I've started another poem on the same topic and invite you to continue and finish it. For each poemstart, I've given you some hints or clues as to what you might do. Feel free to use my hints or to go off completely in your own direction. I start a lot of my own poems this way. When I am inspired, I jot down a couple of lines in my notebook, having no notion of how to finish the poem. I have lots of fun playing with words and ideas and "solving" the poem. That's what I hope you'll do with the poemstarts in this book. Maybe you'll even be inspired to write poems of your own from scratch. I surely hope so.

Your friend,

Jack Prelutsky

# READ THIS NOW!

I have something important to ask you—
**PLEASE DON'T WRITE IN THIS BOOK.**
It is beautifully printed on very fine paper,
and it would be a shame to scribble in it.
Also, if you write in it, you're likely to ruin
things for someone else. Get yourself a pencil
and a notebook or some scrap paper before
you begin working on the poemstarts.

**MUTTERLY**

My dog's name is Mutterly.
He makes my heart melt, butterly.
I love the mongrel utterly.
—*Tony Johnston*

**A BULLDOG'S FACE**

Nothing on a bulldog's face
Seems to have a proper place
His eyelids droop
His jaws are square
His jowls are beyond compare
His nose looks like he's had a fight
He's got a great big underbite
You look at him and have to hoot
He's so ugly that he's cute
—*Marilyn Singer*

**INTO YOUR LOVING ARMS I LEAP**
Into your loving arms I leap—
Please scratch between my ears.
I love the way you cuddle me
And ease my doggy fears.
—*Amy E. Sklansky*

**DOG POEMSTART**
My dog is less than one foot tall
And hasn't any tail.
She never answers when I call,

- - - - - - - - - - - - - - - - - - - -

There are lots of ways you can continue this poemstart and make the fourth line rhyme with the second. I've given you a few rhyming words to think about. For example, you might write about how your dog is slower than a snail or how it brings the morning mail. You can also continue the poem with different rhyming words of your own.

*some possible rhyming words:*

| | | |
|---|---|---|
| snail | rail | frail |
| pale | trail | mail |
| nail | pail | stale |

## CRACK AN EGG

Crack an egg.
Stir the butter.
Break the yolk.
Make it flutter.
Stoke the heat.
Hear it sizzle.
Shake the salt,
just a drizzle.
Flip it over,
just like that.
Press it down.
Squeeze it flat.
Pop the toast.
Spread jam thin.
Say the word.
Breakfast's in.
—*Denise Rodgers*

## MASHED POTATOES

Mashed potatoes,
mashed potatoes,
piled up high,

mashed potatoes,
mashed potatoes,
up to the sky,

mashed potato clouds,
mashed potato moon,

scoop it all up
with a giant's spoon.
—*Eve Merriam*

6

## FOOD POEMSTART

I'm hungry, so I think that I
Will have a piece of penguin pie.
When that is finished, I will eat
A — — — — — — — — — — — — — — — —

*some possible rhyming words:*

| | | |
|---|---|---|
| **meat** | **beet** | **wheat** |
| **feet** | **seat** | **treat** |
| **sweet** | **sheet** | **neat** |

Just imagine all the ridiculous things
you might eat that rhyme with the
word "eat" . . . there are quite a few.
After you finish the first verse, try
writing more rhyming couplets (pairs
of lines that rhyme) about silly food.

## EATING BLUEBERRIES

We found them
  Big as marbles
And we rolled them
  In our mouths
And bit them
  Till the juice
Ran down in rivers.

We gathered
  And we feasted
Till our teeth
  Turned berry-blue
And now
  Our smiles
Give everyone
  The shivers.
—*Sandra Olson Liatsos*

## IF WE DIDN'T HAVE BIRTHDAYS

If we didn't have birthdays, you wouldn't be you.
If you'd never been born, well then what would you do?
If you'd never been born, well then what would you be?
You *might* be a fish! Or a toad in a tree!
You might be a doorknob! Or three baked potatoes!
You might be a bag full of hard green tomatoes.
Or worse than all that . . . Why, you might be a WASN'T!
A Wasn't has no fun at all. No, he doesn't.
A Wasn't just isn't. He just isn't present.
But you . . . You ARE YOU! And, now isn't that pleasant!
—*Dr. Seuss*

## BIRTHDAY

When he asked for the moon
they laughed
and said
that his birthday wish
was wrong

and the little boy cried
and went
outside
and he looked at the moon
so long

that it floated to where
his eyes
looked up
and it shimmered him
in its light

and the little boy knew
as his wish
came true
that a birthday wish
is right.
—*Myra Cohn Livingston*

**BIRTHDAY POEMSTART**
Tomorrow is my birthday,
And I can hardly wait.
Time is moving much too slow,
I'm in an anxious state.

Tomorrow is my birthday,

There are so many things you could talk about here to continue this poem. You could talk about how wonderful your last birthday was, the presents you got, all the friends that came to your party. You could talk about how you're going to be a whole year older. You could talk about all the cake you're going to eat, or the wish you're going to make, or how you're looking forward to a visit from your favorite aunt or uncle. It's completely up to you.

**BIRTHDAYS**
If birthdays happened once a week
Instead of once a year,
Think of all the gifts you'd get
And all the songs you'd hear
And think how quickly you'd grow up;
Wouldn't it feel queer
If birthdays happened once a week
Instead of once a year?
—*Mary Ann Hoberman*

**UPSIDE DOWN**
It's funny how beetles
and creatures like that
can walk upside down
as well as walk flat.

They crawl on a ceiling
and climb on a wall
without any practice
or trouble at all,

While *I* have been trying
for a year (maybe more)
and still I can't stand
with my head on the floor.
—*Aileen Fisher*

**BUGS**
I am very fond of bugs.
I kiss them
And I give them hugs.
—*Karla Kuskin*

**BUG POEMSTART**
If I were a bug
And I'm glad I'm not,
I'd never roam the street.
I'd do my best
To stay away
From people's giant feet.

If I were a bug,

- - - - - - - - - - - - - - - - - - - - - - - -

Imagine what it would be like to be a bug. You'd be much smaller than you are now, and you'd have six legs. Your whole world would look very different. Can you think of ways to continue this poem from a bug's point of view? Your poem can be silly, serious, or somewhere in between.

**MAYFLY AND JUNE BUG**
Once I saw a Mayfly
Fluttering in the sun,
        As if to say,
        *This must be May!*
But April'd just begun.

And when I met a June Bug
Clicketing in the clover,
        He gave a nod,
        And that was odd,
July was almost over.
—*J. Patrick Lewis*

## MOO

No matter the time,
the place, or season,
with no excuse,
for no known reason,
in the middle of a meadow
a cow says "Moo!"
Then all
the other cows
say it, too.

What does
moo mean,
anyway?
What,
exactly,
are they trying to say?

No matter what else
they're thinking of doing,
if they're cows
they're probably
thinking of mooing.
—*Alice Schertle*

## THE COW

The cow mainly moos as she chooses to moo
and she chooses to moo as she chooses.

She furthermore chews as she chooses to chew
and she chooses to chew as she muses.

If she chooses to moo she may moo to amuse
or may moo just to moo as she chooses.

If she chooses to chew she may moo as she chews
or may chew just to chew as she muses.
—*Jack Prelutsky*

## THE COW

The cow is of the bovine ilk;
One end is moo, the other, milk.
—*Ogden Nash*

## COW POEMSTART

I am a cow,
And so I moo,
For mooing is
What cows all do.

I moo because

- - - - - - - - - - - - - - - - - - - - - - - - -

Here are three poems about cows, and all of them talk either a little or a lot about mooing. Although there may be cows that don't moo, I've never met one myself.

My poemstart talks about mooing from a cow's point of view. Think of all the reasons why a cow might moo and then try to continue the poem with some of them.

## MY FIRST BEST FRIEND

My first best friend is Awful Ann—
she socked me in the eye.
My second best is Sneaky Sam—
he tried to swipe my pie.
My third best friend is Max the Rat—
he trampled on my toes.
My fourth best friend is Nasty Nell—
she almost broke my nose.

My fifth best friend is Ted the Toad—
he kicked me in the knee.
My sixth best friend is Grumpy Gail—
she's always mean to me.
My seventh best is Monster Moe—
he often plays too rough.
That's all the friends I've got right now—
I think I've got enough.
—Jack Prelutsky

## I REMEMBER, I REMEMBER

I remember, I remember
How we used to play outside,
Running through the tall grass
Finding where to hide,

Chugging through the summertime
Like summer couldn't end:
That's the way we used to play,
Me and my old friend.
—Dennis Lee

## WAIT FOR ME

Wait for me
and I'll be there
and we'll walk home together,
if it's raining
puddle pails
or if it's sunny weather.

Wait for me
and I'll be there
and we'll walk home together.
You wear red
and I'll wear blue,
and we'll be friends forever.
—*Sarah Wilson*

## FRIENDS POEMSTART

I'm lucky, lucky, lucky,
For I like my neighborhood.
I have a lot of friends here,
And all of them are good.

Some of them are serious,
And some of them are _ _ _ _ _ _

_ _ _ _ _ _ _ _ _ _ _ _ _ _ _ _ _ _ _

Here's your chance to talk about your friends. You can talk about why you like them, how long you've known them, the games you play, special times you've had with them—anything that pops into your head. You can even name them and tell us unusual things about them. Don't worry too much about making the poem rhyme—it's more important to express your feelings.

For example, here's another poemstart, one that doesn't rhyme, that you might want to use:

When I'm feeling sad,
I'm glad that I have friends.
I tell them my troubles,
And they always listen.

When I'm feeling happy,
I'm glad that I have friends.

_ _ _ _ _ _ _ _ _ _ _ _ _ _ _ _ _ _ _

**WINTER MORNING**

Winter is the king of showmen,
Turning tree stumps into snow men
And houses into birthday cakes
And spreading sugar over lakes.
Smooth and clean and frosty white,
The world looks good enough to bite.
That's the season to be young,
Catching snowflakes on your tongue.

Snow is snowy when it's snowing,
I'm sorry it's slushy when it's going.
—*Ogden Nash*

**ONE THING I KNOW**
Snow's cold.
Snow's white.
Snow's soft.
Snow's bright.
One thing
I know—
I DO
LIKE SNOW.
—*Ivy O. Eastwick*

**SNOW POEMSTART**
It's snowing on the treetops,
It's snowing on my house.
A mouse is running through the snow,
It's snowing on the mouse.

It's snowing _ _ _ _ _ _ _ _ _ _ _ _

_ _ _ _ _ _ _ _ _ _ _ _ _ _ _ _ _ _

I grew up in New York City, where it snowed a lot almost every winter. I loved playing in the snow—making snowmen, having snowball fights, making angels in the snow, having all sorts of fun in the snow. I still like snow, but now when it snows at my house, I have to shovel it. I don't like that at all.

Have fun with this poemstart—just imagine all the things that the snow might be falling on and put them in.

**FOOTPRINTS**
We went out, and in the night
All the world had turned to white.
Snowy garden, snowy hedge,
Ice along the window ledge.
And all around the garden seat
A tiny bird with tiny feet
Had left his footprints in the snow,
As he went hopping to and fro.
—*Shirley Hughes*

**THE BOX TURTLE**
This bony dome's
My mobile home,
A shell
So swell
In which to roam.
And when I'm scared
By bear or fox,
Inside I hide
Safe in my box.
I close it shut
And go to bed,
Secure from beasts
That *box* my head.
—Douglas Florian

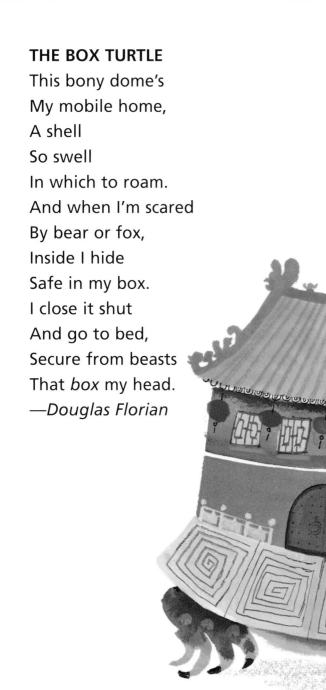

**A TURTLE WITH A TINY HEAD**
A turtle with a tiny head
And little streaks of Chinese red
Came trotting gaily to the lawn
One summer day at early dawn.

I tapped him lightly with a stick.
He drew his head and legs in, quick.
Strange turtle with your streaks of red.
And folding legs and hiding head!
—Effie Lee Newsome

## TURTLE POEMSTART

Because I am a turtle,
A shell protects my hide.
Because I am a turtle,
I feel secure inside.

Because I am a turtle,

- - - - - - - - - - - - - - - - -

There are many ways to continue this poem. For example, you might talk more about the shell, or about how slowly the turtle moves, or about how it likes to spend its time. You also might write about some of the things a turtle can't do, such as run, jump, or turn somersaults.

Every other line of the poem does not have to be "Because I am a turtle." For example, here is one way that I continued my own turtle poemstart:

I keep my head and tail in
Whenever danger's near
And never stick my neck out
Until the coast is clear.

## TURTLE TROUBLE

Tell me if you think you know
How to make a turtle go.
I've pushed, I've tapped,
I've really tried—
But mine, I think,
Is stuck inside!
—*Charles Ghigna*

19

**LET'S COUNT THE RAINDROPS**
Let's count the raindrops
as they pour:
one million, two million,
three million, four.
—*Alan Benjamin*

**RAIN**
Summer rain
  is soft and cool,
  so I go barefoot
  in a pool.

But winter rain
  is cold, and pours,
  so I must watch it
  from indoors.
—*Myra Cohn Livingston*

**RAIN POEMSTART**
The rain is falling pitter-pat,
And I am sitting with my cat
And peering out a windowpane,
Delighted by the gentle rain.

The rain – – – – – – – – – – – –
– – – – – – – – – – – – – – – –

I live in a part of the country where it rains a lot—in fact, it's raining while I'm writing this . . . so I've had lots of chances to look at the rain, and listen to the rain, and think about the rain, and walk in the rain, and run really fast to get out of the rain. Write down some of your own experiences with rain and try to continue this poemstart with some of them. You might write about how you feel when it rains, or how there are things you can or can't do when it rains.

**TO WALK IN WARM RAIN**
To walk in warm rain
    And get wetter and wetter!
To do it again—
To walk in warm rain
    Till you drip like a drain.
To walk in warm rain
    And get wetter and wetter.
—David McCord

## RUNNING AWAY

Running away
From the rest of today
Running away
From you
Running away
From "Don't do that"
From all of the things
I must constantly do.
I feel too tall
I feel too old
For a hundred helpings of being told.
Packing my head
Taking my feet
Galloping down the familiar street.
My head is a bird.
My heart is free again.
I might come back
When I feel like me again.
—*Karla Kuskin*

## A CIRCLE OF SUN

I'm dancing.
I'm leaping.
I'm skipping about.
I gallop.
I grin.
I giggle.
I shout.
I'm Earth's many colors.
I'm morning and night.
I'm honey on toast.
I'm funny.
I'm bright.
I'm swinging.
I'm singing.
I wiggle.
I run.
I'm a piece of the sky
in a circle of sun.
—*Rebecca Kai Dotlich*

## MYSELF POEMSTART
I'm bigger than a bumblebee,
I'm smaller than a whale.
I'm slower than a cheetah,
I'm faster than a snail.

I'm _ _ _ _ _ _ _ _ _ _ _ _ _ _ _ _ _

This should be easy and fun, for if there's one thing that you really know about, it's yourself. Make a list of as many things about yourself as you can think of and then try to continue this poem with some of those things. Be as creative and as silly as you want. Try comparing yourself with some other animals . . . for example, are you stronger than an elephant?

## LONELY
When I feel lonely
    Then I sit
All by myself
    And think a bit,
And ask myself
    Why is it true
That certain times
    I feel so blue?
—*William Wise*

## Grateful acknowledgment is made to the following for permission to reprint previously published material:

Boyd's Mill Press, Inc., for "A Circle of Sun" from *Lemonade Sun and Other Summer Poems* by Rebecca Kai Dotlich, copyright © 1998 by Rebecca Kai Dotlich; "One Thing I Know" from *Some Folks Like Cats and Other Poems* by Ivy O. Eastwick, compiled by Walter B. Barbe, copyright © 2002 by Highlights for Children, Inc.; "Eating Blueberries" from *Bicycle Riding and Other Poems* by Sandra Olson Liatsos, copyright © 1997 by Sandra Olson Liatsos; "A Turtle with a Tiny Head" from *Wonders: The Best Children's Poems of Effie Lee Newsome*, compiled by Rudine Sims Bishop, copyright © 1999. Reprinted by permission of Wordsong, Boyd's Mill Press.

Curtis Brown Ltd. for "The Cow," copyright © 1931 by Ogden Nash, renewed; "Winter Morning," copyright © 1962 by Ogden Nash, renewed; "Lonely" from *All on a Summer's Day* (Pantheon, 1971), copyright © 1971 by William Wise. All poems reprinted by permission of Curtis Brown Ltd.

Charles Ghigna for "Turtle Trouble" from *Tickle Day* (Hyperion, 1994), copyright © 1994 by Charles Ghigna. Reprinted by permission of the author.

Harcourt, Inc., for "The Box Turtle" from *Lizards, Frogs, and Polliwogs* by Douglas Florian, copyright © 2001 by Douglas Florian; "Birthdays" from *The Llama Who Had No Pajama: 100 Favorite Poems* by Mary Ann Hoberman, copyright © 1981 by Mary Ann Hoberman; "Mutterly" from *It's About Dogs* by Tony Johnston, copyright © 2000 by The Living Trust of Tony Johnston; "Moo" from *How Now, Brown Cow?* by Alice Schertle, copyright © 1994 by Alice Schertle. All poems reprinted by permission of Harcourt, Inc.

HarperCollins Publishers for "Let's Count the Raindrops" from *A Nickel Buys a Rhyme* by Alan Benjamin, text copyright © 1993 by Alan Benjamin; "Footprints" (U.S. rights) from *Rhymes for Annie Rose* by Shirley Hughes, copyright © 1982 by Shirley Hughes; "I Remember, I Remember" from *Bubblegum Delicious* by Dennis Lee, copyright © 2000 by Dennis Lee; "The Cow" from *Zoo Doings* by Jack Prelutsky, copyright © 1983 by Jack Prelutsky; "My First Best Friend" from *It's Raining Pigs and Noodles* by Jack Prelutsky, copyright © 2000 by Jack Prelutsky. All poems used by permission of HarperCollins Publishers.

Henry Holt and Company for "A Bulldog's Face" from *It's Hard to Read a Map with a Beagle on Your Lap* by Marilyn Singer, text copyright © 1993 by Marilyn Singer; "Into Your Loving Arms I Leap" from *From the Doghouse* by Amy E. Sklansky, text copyright © 2002 by Amy E. Sklansky. All poems reprinted by permission of Henry Holt and Company, LLC.

Little, Brown and Company for "To Walk in Warm Rain" from *Speak Up* by David McCord, copyright © 1979 by David McCord. Reprinted by permission of Little, Brown and Company.

Penguin Group (USA) Inc. for "Mayfly and June Bug" from *Little Buggers: Insect and Spider Poems* by J. Patrick Lewis, illustrated by Victoria Chess, text copyright © 1998 by J. Patrick Lewis. Used by permission of Dial Books for Young Readers, a division of Penguin Young Readers Group, a member of Penguin Group (USA) Inc.

The Random House Group Ltd. for "Footprints" (Canadian rights) from *Rhymes for Annie Rose* by Shirley Hughes, copyright © 1982 by Shirley Hughes. Used by permission of The Random House Group Ltd.

Random House, Inc., for "If We Didn't Have Birthdays" from *Happy Birthday to You!* by Dr. Seuss, TM and copyright © Dr. Seuss Enterprises, L.P. 1959, renewed 1987. Used by permission of Random House Children's Books, a division of Random House, Inc.

Marian Reiner, Literary Agent, for "Upside Down" from *When It Comes to Bugs* by Aileen Fisher; "Birthday" by Myra Cohn Livingston and "Rain" from *A Song I Sang to You* by Myra Cohn Livingston, copyright © 1958, 1959, 1965, 1967, 1969, 1984 by Myra Cohn Livingston; "Mashed Potatoes" from *Higgle Wiggle* by Eve Merriam, copyright © 1994 by The Estate of Eve Merriam. All poems used by permission of Marian Reiner.

Denise Rodgers for "Crack an Egg" from *A Little Bit of Nonsense* (Creative Writing Press, 1998, 2001), copyright © 2001 by Denise Rodgers. Reprinted by permission of the author.

Scott Treimel New York for "Running Away" from *Near the Window Tree*, copyright © 1975, 1980 by Karla Kuskin; "Bugs" from *Alexander Soames: His Poems*, copyright © 1962, 1980 by Karla Kuskin. All poems reprinted by permission of Scott Treimel New York.

Sarah Wilson for "Wait for Me" from *June Is a Tune That Jumps on a Stair* (Simon & Schuster, 1992), copyright © 1992 by Sarah Wilson. Reprinted by permission of the author.

# For Morgan—J.P.
# For Ivy, Derek, and Sebastian—M.S.

Holiday
Reminder
1) Clean up
2) Brush
3) Clear
4) Make
5) Get

Chill out!

Birthday

look up!
Karla Kuskin
Ogden Nash
Marilyn Singer
Charles Ghigna
Dr. Seuss

To walk in
warm
Rain...

will have a penguin
pie
When that is finished, i will
eat
A